FRED HARVEY

Creator of Western Hospitality

Train travel by the turn of the century had become much more comfortable compared to the days when Fred Harvey first rode them. Photo courtesy: Kansas State Historical Society

FRED HARVEY

Creator of Western Hospitality

William Patrick Armstrong

CANYONLANDS

PUBLICATIONS

AN INVITATION FROM THE AUTHOR:

Although Fred Harvey has been gone for nearly a century, many people today are still able to recall interesting stories about him that have been passed down through their families. I encourage the reader to relate any information you feel would be of interest to readers, enabling me to include it in the next edition. You may send that information to:

William Armstrong
^c/o Canyonlands Publications
PO Box 16175
Bellemont, AZ 86015

ACKNOWLEDGMENTS

The author would like to thank the following individuals or organizations for their assistance with this project:

Connie Menninger, Santa Fe Railway Project Archivist, Kansas State Historical Society; Susan McGlothlin of the Special Collections and Archives Department of Northern Arizona University's Cline Library; Michael O'Hara, Associate Librarian & Archivist, Museum of Northern Arizona; Tony Marinella, Photo Archivist, Museum of Northern Arizona; the staff of Flagstaff City/Coconino County Public Library; Lena Kent, Public Affairs, Burlington Northern Santa Fe Railway; Michael W. Blaszak; Lowell Fay, Bright Angel History Room, Grand Canyon; Dennis Reason, AmFac Interpretive Trainer; Canyonlands Publications; and last but not least, my wife and editor, Patrice Armstrong.

Trains continued mail delivery well into the 20th century. Fred Harvey became one of the nation's first railway postal clerks in 1862. Photo courtesy: Kansas State Historical Society

CONTENTS

Frederick Henry Harvey. Photo courtesy: Museum of Northern Arizona Photo Archives

INTRODUCTION

Fred Harvey is a name that may not ring a bell with the average American traveler today. But a century ago, Fred Harvey was a household name, synonymous with high quality food served pleasantly. A person could not travel from coast to coast by train without seeing that name emblazoned on dinnerware, ice cream cartons or signs over dining rooms as they stopped for food along the way.

Fred Harvey's life is the story of the American Dream. That dream is not about someone who inherited millions and lived in grand style. Harvey's life started from financial scratch across the Atlantic. He made his own fortunes the "old-fashioned way" by starting at the bottom of the ladder in the restaurant business as a dishwasher, and rising to the very pinnacle of the tourism and hospitality industry.

The Fred Harvey Company in the late 1800s grew because Harvey himself was passionately devoted to the mission he chose - caring for the American traveler. Traveling for serious distances in those days meant taking the train. Train travel was a miserable, uncomfortable business over bumpy tracks in exposed rail cars with wooden benches for seats. Train passengers were at the mercy of rail employees who cooperated with restauranteurs at the stops to take their money and give them inedible food - or no food at all.

Harvey himself was a victim of those tactics in his business travels. His mission became to provide good food at a fair price, prepared to high standards and graciously served. The product he envisioned became the cornerstone of a business expansion that made Fred Harvey hospitality widespread and respected.

The English-born Harvey offered his employees a respectable line of work for their entire careers, if they chose. Employment as a "Harvey Girl" was one of the first opportunities for women to work in a decent environment with reasonable pay. In return for guaranteed employment, Harvey demanded that his workers adhere to strict standards that ensured a pleasant, memorable experience for every one of his customers.

Life was not easy for Harvey. During his life he survived partners who stole from him, civil war, national depression, and lingering poor health caused by disease. It could have destroyed a lesser person. Setbacks only made Harvey stronger. He experienced real success only after he had passed his fortieth birthday. As you will discover in the following chapters, Fred Harvey's life is the story of the incredible resilience of a strong human spirit.

Because Fred Harvey was not "well-to-do" at birth, or a public figure later on in his life, public records of his existence are few and far between. This is especially true for the first half of his life. Accounts from former employees who had direct contact with Harvey also fall into this category. But company legends of the man continue to be discussed today by those who work within shops, hotels and restaurants operated by AmFac Parks & Resorts, which took over Fred Harvey, Inc. in 1968.

Harvey was a driving force behind America's newborn hospitality industry. While previous books have focused on his famous "Harvey Girls," or the way his company promoted the Southwest to travelers after his death, this book will focus on the life events of the man behind the legend. Harvey rejected failure, passionately devoted himself to his mission, and inspired others to join him on that mission. He is the archetype people like Ray Kroc, J. Willard Marriott, Dave Thomas of Wendy's, and Harland ("Colonel") Sanders instinctively follow. Fred Harvey was an American first. As we pass into the new millenium, this is an effort to make sure he is not forgotten.

Fred Harvey
by William Patrick Armstrong

chapter one

BEGINNING IN ENGLAND

A drive down any highway in America carries the promise of convenient dining on the road. Signs displaying colorful logos of popular fast food restaurants are an early warning system for drivers that it's time to make a decision: What will they eat to satisfy their craving of the moment?

In most cases, travelers can get exactly what they desire from a variety of national chain restaurants operating in towns and cities of any measurable population. These traveling patrons rarely encounter any unpleasant surprises on the menus of these eateries, as each restaurant subscribes to a standard that is closely observed by every franchise operator and frequently checked by a corporate-level manager. A McDonald's®, for example, will serve its customers the same Big Mac® in Deming, New Mexico, that is served in Miami, Florida. A standard exists for everything involved in getting that Big Mac® into the customer's hands: from the friendly greeting of the cashier, to the amount of a burger's cooking time, to the exact ingredients used in its preparation.

Customers know that standard exists, but have grown so accustomed to it that they often take that standard for granted. Where did these chain restaurant standards come from? The answer to that question can be found more than a century ago by investigating the lifetime work of one man—Fred Harvey, the pioneer of American travel food service.

Frederick Henry Harvey was born on June 27, 1835. Little is known about his father, Charles, who may have been a tailor. His mother, Helen Manning Harvey, was believed to have been of Scottish descent. Details for young Fred's life are very sketchy, though he is thought to have been baptized in the Church of England at St. Martin's in the Fields church in London.

The time and place young Fred was born into was remarkable for its widespread misery and disease. Living in London in the first half of the nineteenth century was motivation enough for many people to purchase a ticket to America for a better life.

Throughout England, an economy once alive with family-owned farms was rapidly becoming industrialized. The demand for craft work was declining, replaced by factory work. As a result of the vanishing family farm and growing manufacturing industry, urban populations swelled. Jobs could be found in smokey towns where textile mills and factories churned out their products at a seemingly endless pace. Many moved to London, which by 1820 already had grown to nearly 1.1 million residents, about a third of England's entire urban population.

Three years before Fred Harvey was born, a combination of an inadequate drinking water supply and poor sanitation services opened the door for a cholera epidemic that swept across England in 1832, killing 31,000 people. When the breadwinner of a household died, often his family was forced to move to the poorhouse. The epidemic was called "the revenge of the working class," as it killed not only those at the bottom of the income ladder, but their employers, too. Wealthy Londoners were surrounded by servants and tradesmen, so disease spread easily.

Times were tough, and even though industrialization was building momentum with new inventions to aid manufacturers, families struggled just to make ends meet. One of those was the Harvey family.

Lured by the promise of America, in 1850, at the age of 15, Fred Harvey boarded a sailing ship bound for New York. Family legend says Fred had only two English pounds in his pocket for the voyage.

chapter two

LEARNING ABOUT AMERICA

By leaving England, Fred Harvey was taking a great risk. Many people before him had made the same voyage in hopes of finding "greener pastures" and the endless opportunities in America. Instead, roughly one-quarter to one-third of those who left their homelands got back onto ships a short time later and returned home. A number of those, however, were seasonal travelers who made the voyage across the Atlantic once a year in order to earn enough money to feed a family back in Europe.

The cost of sailing to America was not prohibitive in the mid-19th century, but the cost actually decreased in the second half of the century. America was exporting bulky raw materials, such as timber, cotton and grain, to European markets. The linens, china and wines sent back on the same ships for the return voyage to America left plenty of room for passengers who were tough enough to endure a steerage-class ticket.

Finding work in New York City was easy enough for the hard-working Harvey. His first job there was as a dishwasher at the Smith and McNeill Cafe at 229 Washington Street. That job paid $2 per week, but it was the work experience that probably helped Harvey more than anything else. If learning the restaurant business from the ground up was what he wanted, Harvey got his wish.

Little time passed before Harvey saved enough money to continue his American journey, this time traveling to New Orleans. His timing could not have been worse. Harvey was able to secure restaurant jobs in New Orleans, but the Yellow Fever epidemic of 1853 swept through soon after his arrival, killing 40,000 people. Harvey contracted the fever, but he recovered. He then moved north to St. Louis.

In 1855, at age 20, Harvey found work as a jeweler and merchant tailor in St. Louis. Two years later, he found a partner to help him establish his first business—a dining hall. A year later, on July 27, 1858, Harvey had decided America truly was the land of opportunity and became a United States citizen.

Harvey's life was changing rapidly. He married 17-year-old Barbara Sarah Mattas on Jan. 14, 1860. Barbara, whose nickname was Sally, was the daughter of Martin Mattas, a Missourian of Bohemian descent who later died of pneumonia in St. Louis as a Union soldier during the Civil War. Together, Sally and Fred would have seven children, five of which survived to adulthood.

The Harveys began their marriage better off than most, with nearly $800 in assets and the dining hall business he shared with his partner.

Up to this point, life had been an uphill struggle for Fred Harvey, and things weren't about to change. When the Civil War broke out in 1861, the Harveys soon discovered that St. Louis was a focal point of division. A United States arsenal was located there, and a battle over control of the arsenal resulted in 28 dead. Harvey was a union sympathizer, but his partner had sided with the confederates. With the Civil War heating up, his partner reportedly absconded with the business assets, leaving Harvey broke and discouraged. At the same time, Harvey came down with another major illness - typhoid.

But in a pattern he repeated several times during his life, Harvey was quick to rebound. He was about to discover the second greatest business influence in his career: Railroads.

Framed portrait of Fred and Sarah Harvey. Photo courtesy: Museum of Northern Arizona Photo Archives

chapter three

EXPLORING THE RAILROADS

Never one to stay down in a rut, Harvey got back on his feet by working for Captain Rufus Ford's Missouri River Packet Line, a railroad that ran tracks from St. Louis to Omaha, Nebraska. After a short stint there, he was hired to work as a mail clerk for John L. Bittinger, the postmaster of St. Joseph, Missouri. This seemingly insignificant postal job proved to be a pivotal move for Harvey.

Just two years earlier, rapid overland mail service had begun opening communication lines across the West. The Pony Express received mail at the Missouri River, then carried it in leather pouches on horseback all the way to California. Mail volume steadily increased, and the Civil War only added to the volume of letters and packages that were being trotted across the trails.

In order to speed up mail delivery, W.A. Davis, the chief mail clerk in St. Joseph, Mo., proposed sorting the mail enroute to eastern points to save time. A mobile post office would allow clerks to have all of their mail sorted by the time it reached the Mississippi River. This rolling postal service officially began on July 26, 1862, on the route between St. Joseph and Quincy, Illinois.

Fred Harvey became one of the two first mobile mail clerks. Having gotten a taste for the railroad life, Harvey moved on to join the Hannibal and St. Joseph line a short time later. This particular line was branded by early travelers as the "Horrible and Slow Jolting" for the uncomfortable ride they endured over rough tracks.

By 1865, with the end of the Civil War, Harvey had advanced to the position of General Western Agent for the North Missouri Railroad, and was transferred 30 miles south to Leavenworth, Kansas.

Going south was a welcome move for the Harvey family. They had recently lost two infant sons to scarlet fever while living in St. Joseph. A fresh start in Leavenworth was marked on March 7, 1866, with the birth of another son, Ford Ferguson Harvey. Ford

The Harvey home in Leavenworth, Kansas, where Harvey's son, Ford, was born in 1866. Photo courtesy: Museum of Northern Arizona Photo Archives

would later become the first "college man" in the Harvey family by attending Racine College in Racine, Wisconsin. Ford would later be forced to drop out of school in 1884 to learn the family business due to his father's failing health.

In 1870, as railroad spikes were being pounded into the dusty earth at a ferocious rate to lay new track, cattle ranching was becoming a booming business in the West.

Texas cattlemen were making good use of the largest spread of free pasture left — the Great Plains. Each spring, cowboys rounded up their herds, branded and castrated the calves, doctored sick animals and prepared themselves and their full-grown steers for the long drive to the nearest railroad.

The risks of the cattle ranching business were tremendous. Rustlers could be hiding in wait and ready to strike at anytime. Cowboys also had to be very careful in planning the drive to allow plenty of pasture grazing along the way. Otherwise, steers would arrive at the market underweight, and less beef meant less money. Fattening up a skinny steer once it was already at market could quickly eat up any profits.

Virtually all livestock driven up the Texas cattle trails passed by rail through Kansas before going on to Eastern markets. Fred Harvey spotted this interchange as a golden opportunity, and he had already proven he was not afraid to take a risk or two.

Harvey had studied the cattle industry while serving as a general agent for the Burlington railroad lines. In fact, Harvey's knowledge of and interest in the cattle business prompted him to buy his own cattle ranch in 1867, gaining even more experience with cowpunchers and cattle sales.

A year later, in 1868, Harvey branched out in his business interests by investing in a new hotel in Ellsworth, Kansas. Ellsworth was experiencing an economic boom. By 1872, the town boasted the largest cattle yards in the state.

Not satisfied with his railroad, cattle ranch and hotel duties, Harvey decided he could also handle the duties of newspaper advertising salesman in the early 1870s. He was hired by the Leavenworth-based Times and Conservative and sometimes pulled in as much as $15,000 in advertising revenues for publisher Dan Anthony while on trips back East. The experience deepened his knowledge of business and how it worked, as well as making it possible for Harvey to make important contacts.

The Santa Fe Railway train depot in Topeka, Kansas. The second story of this depot was where Fred Harvey opened his first railway lunchroom in 1876. The lunchroom closed its doors in 1940. Photo courtesy: Museum of Northern Arizona Photo Archives

chapter four

SEEING THE NEED

Times were good and getting better for Harvey. Up to this point, he had worked for the Hannibal and St. Joseph Railroad, the North Missouri Railroad, and the Chicago, Burlington and Quincy Railroad. All three railroads were initially separate companies, but were later absorbed by the "Joy System," the first large Western railroad ownership group.

Railroad magnate James F. Joy of Detroit was at the helm of this group, which proved to be loosely knit and overbuilt. The Joy System disintegrated rapidly during the Panic of 1873, a national depression that ran many businesses into the ground.

Despite economic depression, Harvey drove on pursuing his dreams. Getting from Leavenworth to east coast business centers forced him to ride a lot of trains, which resulted in a multitude of uncomfortable and regrettable trips.

Trains at that time were the fastest, safest way to travel from coast to coast. But a train ride then was nothing like the smooth, climate-controlled ride of today. Passengers had to sit on hard wooden bench seats. Some coaches were fully enclosed, but their loose-fitting windows offered little protection against the engine's soot and cinders, not to mention bad weather.

Only the deepest sleepers got any rest on a train trip. Travelers were often jarred by rough stretches of poorly laid track, or they were awakened by the noise of animals that were allowed to travel in the same coaches with people.

Some cars, known as "Zulu" cars, were even less comfortable. Zulu cars were constructed of two sections containing double berths made of wooden slats that rested over a narrow aisle. Travelers in these cars padded the slats with their own blankets or clothing. A cooking stove at one end of the Zulu car was where passengers prepared their meals during a longer trip. Those who did not prepare their own meals were at the mercy of eating establishments at stops along the way.

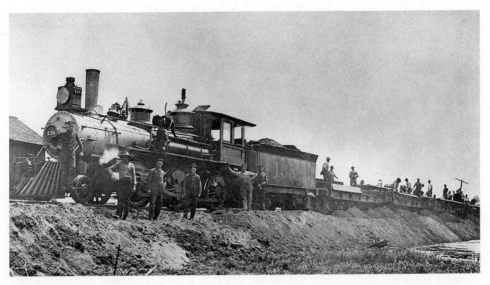

The job of laying track for a new railway line required the work of many strong backs and cooperative weather. Photo courtesy: Museum of Northern Arizona Photo Archives

Harvey detested these miserable, track-side eateries. Passengers were often served vile, greasy stew. Meat was usually fried to conceal its age, and bacon was often rancid. Pie, if offered, was one of the dried fruit and crust variety. Eggs offered a new, disgusting taste sensation for passengers because they had been preserved in lime many days earlier.

The unfortunate train travelers washed their meals down with a cup of bitter coffee, which sometimes had been brewed an entire week earlier and simply reheated for each arriving trainload of patrons.

Many passengers avoided stomach disorders by packing their own box lunches which included cheese, fruit and bread, and hoped their supply would hold out until they reached their destinations. Passengers had heard about the cruel treatment they would receive at the hands of train employees if they ran out of their own food.

Some conniving trainmen would take the food orders and payment from passengers before they pulled into the station, and then would act as if they were calling their orders ahead by telegraph so the food would be ready. They would then wait until their passengers were just about to be served these meals to announce that the train was pulling away from the station. This action forced passengers to leave their meals uneaten, but paid for in advance. Trainmen then split the profits with unscrupulous restaurant operators all along the line.

Those "fortunate" to enjoy their meals might have wished that they, too, had fasted. One Englishman wrote the following about his train travels across the American West: "Hurried, degraded, and miserable, you rush back into your carriage after paying some three shillings for a revolting meal." Another traveler suggested that "trains acted as if ashamed of something they had done, so silent was their departure."

Harvey soon caught onto this seemingly nationwide scheme to swindle train travelers and he took action in 1875. Harvey and a partner, J.P. "Jeff" Rice, opened two eating houses that year along the Kansas Pacific Railroad, with one at Wallace, Kansas and the other in Hugo, Colorado.

Their restaurants thrived, but Harvey didn't want to stop there. He envisioned opening many more across the West. Rice did not see eye-to-eye with Harvey, especially when it came to Harvey's high standards for each restaurant. After all, the public was used to a lower level of service and an equally lower level of food quality. But at least this time, the split between partners was fair and above-board. Harvey and Rice divided their profits, leaving Harvey the operation to himself.

A Fred Harvey lunchroom in Rincon, New Mexico. Photo courtesy: Kansas State Historical Society

chapter five

PUTTING IT ALL TOGETHER

Harvey then presented his ideas of expansion to his bosses at the Burlington line, but the depression had left them leary of new investments and potential risks. Instead, the Burlington bosses directed Harvey across the tracks to the Santa Fe Railroad.

In 1876, the Santa Fe was one of the fastest expanding railroads in the country, under the leadership of Thomas Nickerson. The Santa Fe had already established a food service for its passengers with restaurant operator Peter Cline on the second floor of its Topeka, Kansas, depot. Cline's meals were described as adequate, but not exceptional. At Harvey's first meeting with Nickerson, he told the railroad president he could personally change railway dining's miserable reputation to something travelers actually looked forward to. The two men reached a "gentlemen's agreement" with a handshake and launched America's first large restaurant chain.

In the spring of 1876, Harvey completed his negotiations with Peter Cline and closed the Topeka lunchroom for 48 hours. In that short amount of time, Harvey scrubbed everything in sight, then brought in new silver and linen. He also upgraded the menu with high quality food, and hired a new manager, Guy Potter. A friend of Harvey's from Leavenworth, Potter already knew the soon-to-be-famous "Harvey Standard." Under Harvey's watchful eye, the pair quickly transformed the lunchroom into a first-class dining facility.

For 35 cents, Harvey's customers would get a breakfast of steak, eggs, hash browns, a stack of six wheat pancakes with maple syrup, and apple pie with coffee for dessert. Harvey's food service was so good that his reputation spread like wildfire.

On January 1, 1878, Harvey signed his first formal contract with the Santa Fe. A short time later, Harvey decided he wanted to expand into the hotel business, as well. The Clifton Hotel was already on the Santa Fe line in Florence, Kansas. Harvey got a good look at the Clifton and wanted the railroad to buy it. For his part, Harvey would serve fine food within it.

But the Santa Fe had its money tied up in a fight with the Denver & Rio Grande Railroad, and told Harvey that if he bought it, they would take it off his hands when conditions permitted. The deal was finalized with the hotel's former owners six months later. Harvey was now the proud owner of his first restaurant and hotel combination.

The excitement of this venture pushed Harvey to new heights. He went all out to make this the best establishment in the region. Harvey hired a Chicago chef for the then unheard-of salary of $5,000 a year. That was twice the annual pay of the next wealthiest man in Florence, the local banker.

This bold move would become a trademark for Harvey, who later hired several well-known chefs from around the world. Many years later, for example, when the son of Germany's Kaiser Wilhelm visited La Fonda Hotel in Santa Fe, he was surprised as he looked up from his table at Chef Konrad Allgaier, who had once cooked in his grandfather's kitchen.

As the Santa Fe stretched westward, passengers such as these gentlemen enjoyed longer rides and a chance to discuss business or trade tales to pass their time between points. Photo courtesy: Kansas State Historical Society

Once again, Harvey brought in fine Irish linen and sparkling English silver to make the Clifton Hotel's restaurant a first-class operation. The Clifton Hotel, also known as the Florence Harvey House, became a template for future dealings with the Santa Fe. The same contract terms agreed upon for the Clifton were the pattern for many more restaurants and/or hotels in the future expansion of the Fred Harvey Company.

In December 1878, the Santa Fe laid track over the snowy Raton Pass into northern New Mexico as it continued its westward push. It was here in the little mountain town of Raton that a late night brawl in about 1883 marked the beginning of one of Harvey's more-famous trademarks, "the Harvey Girl."

The chain of events began one evening when the Raton Harvey House's all-male staff was cut to ribbons in an after-hours fight. As a result, the entire crew was unable to report to work the next morning. Word of the incident enraged Harvey, who immediately fired the staff, as well as the manager.

His new manager in Raton, Tom Gable, replaced the rambunctious men with attractive young women. Gable correctly believed these women would be more reliable on the job and get in much less trouble in their free time.

Gable took a gamble and he was right. The entire community found the new staff to be very charming and much more dignified than the original crew. Harvey also took notice and soon after began running newspaper and magazine advertisements to attract more Harvey Girls for his other facilities.

The ads called for "young women 18 to 30 years of age, of good character, attractive and intelligent," to move to the West for employment. He set up a Chicago employment office, screened applicants, and placed them all along the Santa Fe line. Applicants who accepted jobs agreed to some unusual contract terms that lasted six, nine or twelve months.

The women had to obey employee rules, follow instructions, travel where needed and perhaps most importantly, agree not to get married for the duration of their first contract. Harvey Girls worked seven days a week for their room and board. They were paid $30 a month for spending money and also given a rail pass once a year that would take them anywhere the Santa Fe chugged along its tracks. In most cases, the girls used their rail passes to return home for visits.

Harvey Girls were issued uniforms that included trim black skirts, shirtwaists, stockings, shoes, ties, and high, white bib aprons. White uniforms were to be worn while serving breakfast and lunch. Black uniforms with starched white aprons were reserved for the serving of dinner. The young women slept in dormitories monitored by house

A Harvey Girl pours fresh coffee in the lunch room at the El Oritz Harvey House, built by the A.T. & S.F Railway in Lamy, New Mexico. Photo courtesy: Northern Arizona University Cline Library

mothers who kept strictly enforced curfews. Over time, as many as 20,000 of these Harvey Girls married ranchers, cowboys, miners, merchants and railroad men. With their education, good manners and strong character, the Harvey Girls truly helped settle the West.

William E. Curtis, a newspaper columnist with the Chicago Record, wrote on May 9, 1899, "Fred Harvey, a remarkable man who has been running the eating stations on the Santa Fe Railway ever since it was built, is responsible for a great deal of growth and a great deal of happiness in this part of the country. He has done more than any immigration society to settle up the Southwest, and still continues to provide wives for ranchmen, cowboys, railway hands and other honest pioneers." Curtis went on to write that "...the successful results of his matrimonial bureau are found in every community."

Better-built passenger cars allowed people of all ages to travel west in safety and comfort by the end of the 19th century. Gone were the bone-shaking, drafty cars and soot-covered passengers that Fred Harvey witnessed as a young immigrant 50 years earlier Photo courtesy: Kansas State Historical Society

Many people assume Fred Harvey was the first to build a large company centered around female labor. However, Harvey was, consciously or not, taking his lead from Francis Cabot Lowell, who took similar action half a century earlier in Waltham, Massachusetts.

Lowell opened a textile mill there in 1813 and recruited area farm girls as his labor force. This New England entrepreneur viewed women as "educated and virtuous" and believed correctly that most would stay on the job long enough to earn a handsome dowry before getting married.

In return, Lowell promised their parents that their daughters would live in a healthy, moral environment. Lowell even went so far as to urge parents to visit their daughters and see for themselves what a fine choice they had made. The young women liked the idea of working at the mill because it gave them their first opportunity to become self sufficient and no longer be a burden on their families.

Just as Harvey would do fifty years later, Lowell set up boarding houses for his female workers, staffing each with "no-nonsense" dorm mothers. Many of his workers were just 15 years old when they started at the mill, leaving in their early twenties. They worked as weavers, carders and spinners for 75 hours over six-day weeks. Their relatively short length of stay suited Lowell, who not only expected them to leave by then, but hoped they would. Lowell welcomed the high turnover rate because he believed that the rigors of mill work made employees less productive after just a few years steady work.

Unlike Harvey, however, Lowell paid lower wages than other employers of his time. But in his defense, his charges for room and board were modest, allowing his employees to save about two dollars per week. A few years of steady savings amounted to an adequate dowry.

But even Lowell cannot take full credit for setting up this nontraditional labor force. Just a few years before he gathered enough funds to build his own mill, Lowell visited Scotland and watched the nimble fingers of young boys working in mills there to create fine textiles. Lowell's staffing formula would be finely honed for even greater success when Fred Harvey adopted it with more generous terms.

chapter six

SETTING THE STANDARD

By July 1879, the Santa Fe had reached Las Vegas, New Mexico, and entered Albuquerque nine months later. Tracks went down in Pinta, Arizona in July 1881, and then on to Needles, California, in April 1883, thereby establishing a West Coast link by way of the Southern Pacific Railroad. History was made on May 31, 1887, when the first Santa Fe train rolled into Los Angeles on exclusively Santa Fe track.

Just seven years after opening his lunchroom in Topeka, Harvey managed 17 eating establishments on the Santa Fe's main line. By the mid-1880s, Harvey House service had become a science. The standard was set, and the reputation was growing.

A special code was developed to streamline this service. A train conductor walked from car to car to take passengers' meal orders. He then gave his list to the engineer, who blasted his whistle code.

The code was heard and interpreted many miles ahead by the Harvey House staff. On some lines, Harvey cooks and waitresses were notified by telegraph of the numbers of hungry passengers who would soon arrive in the lunchroom. Harvey Houses served at least two and sometimes three train meals a day. Trains stopped for a maximum of 30 minutes at each stop.

When the train pulled into the depot, the Harvey House manager greeted them by banging a gong, prompting the Harvey Girls to serve the first course of the meal under the watchful eye of the head waitress, or "wagon boss."

The dining room manager also made a point of walking among his patrons and assuring them that they could take their time and enjoy their meal. This was something of obvious importance to their ultimate boss, Fred Harvey, who was rushed through too many meals on earlier train rides. In a dining room, which was somewhat fancier than a lunchroom, men were required to wear jackets. Those without were provided jackets. This caused some heated discussions in more rustic "cow towns" further west.

Santa Fe dining cars were able to serve good meals thanks to a well-planned and well-equipped kitchen that rolled on the rails with them. Photo courtesy: Kansas State Historical Society

Harvey's sky-high standards were brought to the attention of his employees through many surprise visits. Substandard managers were fired on the spot. One legend has Harvey tossing over improperly set tables in order to emphasize his point about high standards.

During an unannounced inspection, Harvey poured over house accounts and food orders. He pulled out a white handkerchief to run along window sills, counter tops and pantry boards. Harvey paid special attention to china and glassware for chips or cracks.

Harvey also taught future inspectors how to do this job properly, according to Joseph A. Noble, author of From Cab to Caboose: Fifty Years of Railroading. "Some Harvey inspections reminded me of the Army," wrote Noble.

"The superintendent didn't just glance in the kitchen, greet the chef, and inquire after his health. He looked the place over as if he suspected a murder had been committed and the search was on for clues. If he found a pitcher of orange juice in the refrigerator, you would think they were about to serve the guests arsenic. Orange juice was to be squeezed out as needed so it would be fresh. Storing it in the refrigerator for use later was an intolerable attempt to get out of a little work."

Each Harvey House had a fairly large staff which typically included a manager, a chef, a head waitress, between 15 and 30 Harvey Girls, a baker, a butcher, several assistant cooks and pantry girls, a housemaid and busboys.

Harvey insisted on the highest quality food and ensured freshness by purchasing much of it from local producers in the form of quail, prairie chickens, butter and vegetables. In those days, local Harvey House managers were able to buy quail at 75-cents a dozen, prairie chickens for one dollar a dozen, and butter at ten cents a pound.

Not all Harvey Houses looked alike. Many were simple, frame houses. In more desolate parts of New Mexico and Arizona, Harvey Houses were sometimes railroad boxcars, but had the same Harvey House standards on the inside, with clean linen, bright silverware and good food.

Expansion of the Harvey House chain brought in the need for help with management. One person could only make so many visits and inspections. Harvey hired two Canadian brothers, David and Harry Benjamin, to assist him. He also hired Byron Schermerhorn to run the chain that had spread to central California by 1887.

These moves gave Harvey more time to seek out more expansion opportunities. He soon took over several small lunchrooms and hotels along the Atlantic and Pacific Railroad, and instructed David Benjamin to bring them up to the Harvey standard, which he did successfully. At the request of Santa Fe vice-president G. W. Smith, Harvey added houses in Arizona and California. From that point on, Harvey operated every single lunch counter, dining room, and hotel in the entire Santa Fe system.

Guests could choose the following from the 75-cent dinner menu on westbound Santa Fe passenger trains in 1888:

Blue Point Oysters on the Half Shell • English Peas Au Gratin •
Filets of Whitefish, Madeira Sauce • Potatoes Francaise
Young Capon, Hollandaise Sauce • Roast Sirloin of Beef au jus •
Pork with Applesauce • Salami of Duck • Queen Olives • Mashed Potatoes
Boiled Sweet Potatoes • Elgin Sugar Corn • Turkey Stuffed • Cranberry Sauce
Baked Veal Pie English Style • Charlotte of Peaches, Cognac Sauce
Prairie Chicken, Currant Jelly • Lobster Salad au Mayonnaise • Sugar Cured Ham
Pickled Lamb's Tongue • Beets • Celery • French Slaw • Apple Pie •
Cold Custard a la Chantilly • Mince Pie • Assorted Cakes • Bananas •
New York Ice Cream • Oranges • Catawba • Wine Jelly • Grapes
Edam and Roquefort Cheese & Bent's Water Crackers • French Coffee

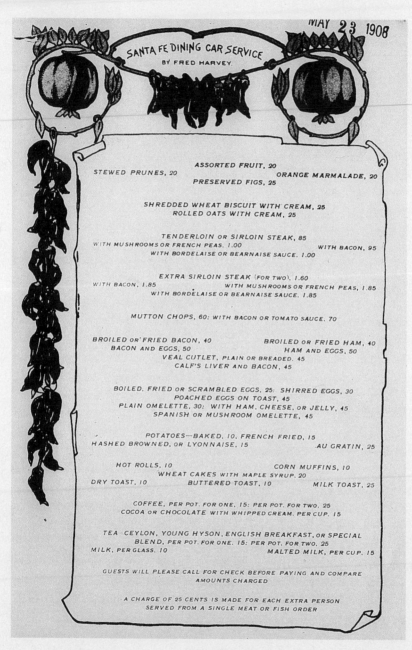

SANTA FE DINING CAR SERVICE
BY FRED HARVEY.

MAY 23 1908

ASSORTED FRUIT, 20
STEWED PRUNES, 20   ORANGE MARMALADE, 20
PRESERVED FIGS, 25

SHREDDED WHEAT BISCUIT WITH CREAM, 25
ROLLED OATS WITH CREAM, 25

TENDERLOIN OR SIRLOIN STEAK, 85
WITH MUSHROOMS OR FRENCH PEAS, 1.00   WITH BACON, 95
WITH BORDELAISE OR BEARNAISE SAUCE, 1.00

EXTRA SIRLOIN STEAK (FOR TWO), 1.60
WITH BACON, 1.85   WITH MUSHROOMS OR FRENCH PEAS, 1.85
WITH BORDELAISE OR BEARNAISE SAUCE, 1.85

MUTTON CHOPS, 60: WITH BACON OR TOMATO SAUCE, 70

BROILED OR FRIED BACON, 40   BROILED OR FRIED HAM, 40
BACON AND EGGS, 50   HAM AND EGGS, 50
VEAL CUTLET, PLAIN OR BREADED, 45
CALF'S LIVER AND BACON, 45

BOILED, FRIED OR SCRAMBLED EGGS, 25: SHIRRED EGGS, 30
POACHED EGGS ON TOAST, 45
PLAIN OMELETTE, 30: WITH HAM, CHEESE, OR JELLY, 45
SPANISH OR MUSHROOM OMELETTE, 45

POTATOES—BAKED, 10, FRENCH FRIED, 15
HASHED BROWNED, OR LYONNAISE, 15   AU GRATIN, 25

HOT ROLLS, 10   CORN MUFFINS, 10
WHEAT CAKES WITH MAPLE SYRUP, 20
DRY TOAST, 10   BUTTERED TOAST, 10   MILK TOAST, 25

COFFEE, PER POT. FOR ONE, 15: PER POT. FOR TWO, 25
COCOA OR CHOCOLATE WITH WHIPPED CREAM, PER CUP, 15

TEA–CEYLON, YOUNG HYSON, ENGLISH BREAKFAST, OR SPECIAL
BLEND, PER POT. FOR ONE, 15: PER POT. FOR TWO, 25
MILK, PER GLASS, 10   MALTED MILK, PER CUP, 15

GUESTS WILL PLEASE CALL FOR CHECK BEFORE PAYING AND COMPARE
AMOUNTS CHARGED

A CHARGE OF 25 CENTS IS MADE FOR EACH EXTRA PERSON
SERVED FROM A SINGLE MEAT OR FISH ORDER

A 1908 Santa Fe dining car menu. Photo courtesy: Kansas State Historical Society

Dinner menus from that time period also featured terrapin, antelope, quail, and Harvey's specialty—Kansas City fillet.

Despite the high costs of providing good service and food, the Harvey Company was becoming extremely profitable. An example of just how profitable can be found in a financial statement of the Fred Harvey files from 1886. Company profits totalled $85,776.97, of which $7,476.48 was taken for "wear and tear," for the year.

Of the remaining amount, Byron Schermerhorn and David Benjamin each received 12.5%. Fred Harvey's share was 75%, or an annual salary of more than $58,700.

A contract change with the Santa Fe on May 1, 1889, granted Harvey exclusive rights to manage and operate the eating houses, lunch stands, which the Harvey company owned, leased or was about to lease on any of the Santa Fe's lines west of the Missouri River. But that same year, friction threatened the railroad's relationship with the Harvey Company.

The trouble began when Allen Manvel became the Santa Fe's new president in September 1889. Manvel drew up plans for dining car service west of Kansas City which conspicuously omitted Fred Harvey. In 1891, Harvey got an injunction to prevent this plan from becoming reality, as well as to keep the Santa Fe from bypassing his eating establishments.

The lawsuit dragged on for several years, and over time, Manvel backed away from his plan. Warmer relations were eventually restored, permitting "business as usual." It is interesting to note that the judge who granted the restraining order, W.C. Hook, happened to be a close, personal friend of Harvey and later served as an honorary pallbearer at Harvey's funeral in 1901.

What changed Manvel's mind? Speculation is that he realized what a devastating effect it would have on the Santa Fe if Harvey was no longer involved. Little details had made everything extremely pleasant for Santa Fe passengers, such as the linen and silver purchased by Harvey himself on trips to Belfast and London. Other details included five kinds of wine listed on the menu of the first Santa Fe diner out of Chicago. Unending quality checks (surprise inspections) by Harvey and his management team kept employees along the entire chain on their toes.

Harvey's highly efficient management system was envied by the other major railroads, and in some cases, copied. Two examples were the Union Pacific and the Central Pacific, according to former Fred Harvey Company president Leslie Scott.

Passengers on the Santa Fe ate very well in part because of Harvey's special refrigerated boxcar that rolled down the tracks twice a week between Los Angeles and Kansas

City. The car supplied Harvey Houses with fresh, California fruits and vegetables on the eastbound run, and choice, Kansas City meats on the return trip.

Menus were planned and printed in Kansas City, then distributed along the route, ensuring that Santa Fe passengers would not be forced to eat the same food all the way west. Harvey's coffee was a genuine treat for passengers, a special blend that maintained uniformity all along the line. Santa Fe trains brought in good water to many western towns whose own supplies contained alkali, which could spoil the Harvey coffee's rich flavor.

Harvey also ran his own farms for his milk, butter and eggs. In some cases, he allowed his managers to make wholesale purchases of local vegetables for distribution throughout the network.

Since the opening of his first dining room almost 20 years before, Harvey built a supply organization that serves as a model for chain restaurants today. The food served on his tables was grown or produced on his farms or it met exacting standards unheard of prior to that time. His table settings were made to his design and the linens were woven to his specifications. He had survived a challenge from an unfriendly railroad administration and never wavered in his demand for quality and expectations for service.

But the story of American business is the story of change, and the national economy was cycling downward once more.

chapter seven

HANDING OVER THE REINS

The end of the nineteenth century was rocky for the Santa Fe, just as it was for the rest of the nation. The Santa Fe entered rate wars in the 1890s that dropped passenger fares from Chicago to the West Coast to a low of $15. But by 1900, the round-trip ticket stabilized at $50. The depression of 1893 ruined many businesses and the once-mighty Santa Fe went into receivership on December 23 of that year.

The Atchison, Topeka & Santa Fe Railway was incorporated on Dec. 12, 1895, in order to purchase the Santa Fe Railroad's assets out of receivership. That purchase was completed on Jan. 1, 1896. Edward Payson Ripley became the A.T.&S.F. president. Ripley had already built a strong reputation as a railroad manager, but his claim to fame at that point had been as a key figure in developing the Chicago World's Columbian Exposition of 1893. Ripley was able to reverse the Santa Fe's financial spiral within six months. He had the confidence to take on the giant Southern Pacific Railroad in 1898. Ripley constructed a Santa Fe route to San Francisco, an enormous task completed in 1900. Railroad historian Edward Hungerford later wrote, "Mr. Ripley was recognized as a consummate genius in his profession."

Ripley's management expertise almost went too far at the end of the century. He examined the railroad's operating costs and decided Harvey's dining service was a prime target for the budget knife. His board of directors, however, convinced him to meet directly with Fred Harvey and to retain the food concessionaire at any cost.

After one meeting, Harvey consented to some revisions and signed what would turn out to be his final contract with the Santa Fe on December 6, 1899.

Harvey's life was marked by his remarkable ability to overcome one obstacle after another. But one obstacle proved too big for Fred Harvey. He fought intestinal cancer for more than 15 years, traveling to California and London for the best medical help available. Even surgery could not stave off the painful cancer that attacked him. With

A 1920s view of the El Tovar Hotel at Grand Canyon, Arizona. Photo courtesy: Northern Arizona University Cline Library

his family members at his bedside, Harvey's fight ended in Leavenworth on February 9, 1901, when he died at age 65.

At his funeral, Elbert Hubbard, a popular writer of that time, delivered the eulogy. "Fred Harvey is dead, but his spirit still lives," said Hubbard. "The standard of excellence he set can never go back. He has been a civilizer and benefactor. He has added to the physical, mental, and spiritual welfare of millions. No sermon can equal a Fred Harvey example—no poet can better a Fred Harvey precept. Fred Harvey simply kept faith with the public. He gave pretty nearly a perfect service."

In a last generous gesture to his employees, Harvey's will included a provision stipulating that every person in his employ at the time of his death was to receive a lifetime pension equal to his salary at the time of retirement.

After death, Harvey's good reputation for fine food and service grew even more. The Atchison, Topeka and Santa Fe was happy to promote that reputation in their 1900 travel folder by saying, "The dining service under the management of Fred Harvey is the best in the world."

Fred Harvey's son, Ford Harvey, took over the company reins upon his father's death. Ford Harvey was in charge when the company's crown jewel, the El Tovar Hotel, opened its doors to Grand Canyon visitors on January 14, 1905. Harvey had been dead for nearly four years by that point, but his high standards were alive and well, giving hotel guests the feeling that Harvey never really left the company. For several years, a life-sized portrait of the distinguished looking, English-born gentleman hung near the El Tovar staircase, where it would be seen by every guest on his way to his room. The portrait now hangs in the History Room at Grand Canyon's Bright Angel Lodge.

Ford Harvey continued in his father's footsteps until his own death on Dec. 13, 1928. The torch was then passed to Ford's brother, Byron S. Harvey.

The company continued its growth in the 20th century. During World War II, for example, a whole new generation of Harvey fans was born in the American soldier, sailor or airman. Across America, military personnel frequented Fred Harvey barber shops, gift shops, soda fountains, cigar stands, restaurants and hotels as they moved to new training assignments.

In 1943, the middle of World War II, the Harvey Company began an advertising campaign asking for the civilian public's patience and understanding. The needs of the servicemen - (which the Harvey company referred to collectively as "Private Pringle") came first. Food rationing and shortage of trained personnel could mean a civilian patron might not even be served a meal - but the company promised to return to their high standard of service when "Private Pringle's job is done."

After the war, growth continued, and culminated with the company's change of ownership at the end of 1968 from the Harvey Family to the AmFac Corporation, which continues to operate hotels, restaurants and gift shops in many of the same locations.

Even today, Fred Harvey's contribution to the hospitality and tourism industry is well understood by industry leaders. "Fred Harvey was a legend in the hospitality industry before his time for service and perfection in details, thereby creating the experience of hospitality on wheels for train travelers," said H.P. Rama, Chairman of the American Hotel & Motel Association and Chairman/CEO of JHM Hotels, Inc.

His influence was also felt in the growth and appreciation of the Southwest. Harvey's company developed a marketing campaign which helped travelers to better understand the significance of the Southwest, said Dennis Reason, Interpretive Trainer, AmFac, at Grand Canyon National Park Lodges. "I think what Fred Harvey did was to interpret the Southwest," said Reason. "He gave it an identity and a meaning. He marketed the Southwest for the Santa Fe. Back in those days the trains were competing against each other like the airlines are today for passengers. The Santa Fe sold the exotic character of the Southwest, the scenery, the mesas and buttes, that you could see in postcards. They made it so that passengers would not just be traveling through the Southwest, but would be experiencing an exotic adventure."

Harvey's example and methods are stamped on the American food service, hotel, and travel industry. Fred Harvey was the pattern for charismatic and successful CEOs in the 20th century. His attention to detail and devotion to quality are a tradition now being carried into the 21st century.

U.S. Army tank corps members take a brief rest during World War II after getting off a troop train and before unloading tanks from flat cars. Photo courtesy: Kansas State Hstorical Society

appendix 1
BIBLIOGRAPHY AND SUGGESTED READING

Asbury, Herbert, *The French Quarter*, New York: Garden City Publishing Company, 1938.

Athearn, Robert G., *Westward the Briton*, Lincoln: University of Nebraska Press, 1953.

Beebe, Lucious and Klegg, Charles, Hear the Train Blow. New York: E.P. Dutton and Company, 1952.

Brown, Dee, *Hear that Lonesome Whistle Blow*, New York: Holt, Rinehart and Winston, 1977.

Bryant, Keith L. Jr., *History of the Atchison, Topeka and Santa Fe Railway*, New York: Macmillan Co., 1974.

Catton, Bruce, *The Coming Fury*, New York: Doubleday and Company, 1961.

Henderson, James David, *"Meals by Fred Harvey" A Phenomenon of the Amercian West*, Fort Worth: Texas Christian University Press, 1969.

Herbert, Charles W., *The Fred Harvey Story*, Arizona Highways, Vol. 44: 6, June 1968.

Jones, George E., *Caterer to a Nation*, Adventures in Business, Buena Park, CA., Vol. II, No. 18, Sept. 15, 1945.

Marshall, James, Santa Fe, *The Railroad that Built an Empire*, New York: Random House, 1943.

Morgan, Kenneth O., *The Oxford History of Britain*, Suffolk, England: Oxford University Press, 1988.

Morison, Samuel Eliot, *The Oxford History of The American People*, New York: New American Library and Oxford University Press, 1972.

Noble, Joseph A., *From Cab to Caboose: Fifty Years of Railroading*, Norman: Univeristy of Oklahoma Press, 1964.

Poling-Kemps, Lesley, *The Harvey Girls*, New York: Paragon House, 1989.

Putnam, Nina Wilcox, *"The Harvey Girls—Tamers of the Wild West"* The Amercian Weekly, August 15, 1948.

Reigel, Robert E., *The Story of the Western Railroads*, Lincoln: University of Nebraska Press, 1926.

Schlereth, Thomas J., *Victorian America: Transformations in Everyday Life*, New York: Harper Collins Publishers, 1991.

Sellers, Charles, and May, Henry, *A Synopsis of American History, Volume One*, Chicago: Rand McNally College Publishing, 1976.

Sellers, Charles, and May, Henry, *A Synopsis of American History, Volume Two*, Chicago: Rand McNally College Publishing, 1976.

Sobel, Robert, and Sicilia, David B., The Entrepreneurs: *An American Adventure*, Boston: Houghton Mifflin Company, 1986.

Thomas, Diane H., *The Southwestern Indian Detours*, Phoenix, AZ: Hunter Publishing Co., 1978.

Walker, Robert H., *Life in the Age of Enterprise*, New York: Capricorn Books, 1971.

Waters, Lawrence Leslie, *Steel Trails to Santa Fe*, Lawrence: University of Kansas Press, 1950.

Weigle, Marta, and Babcock, Barbara A., *The Great Southwest of the Fred Harvey Company and the Santa Fe Railway*, Phoenix, AZ: The Heard Museum, 1996.

Zornow, William F., Kansas: *A History of the Jayhawk State*, Norman: University of Oklahoma Press, 1957.

appendix 2
KEY EVENTS TIMELINE

1835 • Frederick Henry Harvey is born in London, England.

1846 • U.S. Army enters Santa Fe, reopening Santa Fe Trail trade after short Mexican embargo.

1848 • Treaty of Guadalupe Hidalgo. Ends Mexican War, with United States paying Mexico $15 million for vast Southwest territory.

1849 • Gold Rush begins at Sutter's Mill in California's Sacramento Valley.

1850 • 15-year-old Fred Harvey sails to America, lands first job as a dishwasher in New York City.

1858 • Harvey becomes a United States citizen.

1860 • Harvey marries Barbara Sarah Mattas. • Abraham Lincoln elected President. • Southern seccession begins with seven states leaving the union. • Cyrus K. Holliday and partners organize the Atchison & Topeka Railroad Company.

1861 • American Civil War breaks out.

1862 • Homestead Act —provides farms of 160 acres to actual settlers. • Morrill Land Grant Act—Land grants to states for agricultural and mechanical colleges • Pacific Railroad Act—Federal subsidies for a railroad from Omaha, Nebraska, to California. • Slavery abolished in the territories and District of Columbia. • The first rolling postal service officially begins on a train route between St. Joseph and Quincy, Illinois.

1863 • Lincoln's Emanicipation Proclamation frees all slaves in Confederate areas • Atchison & Topeka Railroad changes name to Atchison, Topeka & Santa Fe Railroad Company.

1865 • War ends when Gen. Lee surrenders to Gen. Grant at Appamattox Courthouse. • Lincoln assassinated. • Thirteenth Amendment abolishes slavery throughout U.S.

1866 • Ford Ferguson Harvey is born in Leavenworth.

1867 • Fred Harvey buys his own cattle ranch in Kansas.

1868 • Congress authorizes A.T. & S.F. to purchase unallotted lands of Pottawatomie Indian Reservation near Topeka for $1 per acre. Resales to area farmers provides construction capital.

1869 • Golden spike is pounded at Promontory Point, Utah, linking the Central Pacific and Union Pacific railroads to form the first transcontinental railroad connection. • A.T. & S.F.'s first locomotive, 4-4-0 Cyrus K. Holliday, pulls the railroad's first train of two cars over 7 miles of track at Wakarusa, Kansas. Holliday predicts A.T. & S.F. lines will run to Chicago, San Francisco, St. Louis and Mexico City. Over time, most of his predictions come true.

1870 • First Mennonite immigrants from the Ukraine settle on Santa Fe line, cultivating red winter wheat that would become Kansas' staple crop. • A.T. & S.F. completes track to Emporia, Kansas, more than 60 miles from Topeka. • Texas cattle drives provide a new source of railroad traffic.

1872 • A.T. & S.F. track laid to Kansas-Colorado border, securing three-million-acre land grant.

1873 • Financial panic sets off a national depression that would last 6 years.

1874 • Barbed wire patented, marking the beginning of the end for open range cattle drives.

1875 • First use of refrigerated box cars allows railroads to haul fresh meat. • Harvey and a partner, J.P. "Jeff" Rice, open two eating houses that year along the Kansas Pacific Railroad.

1876 • Harvey begins to operate a lunchroom in Topeka, Kansas, for the Santa Fe Railroad based on a handshake.

1878 • Fred Harvey signs his first formal contract with the Santa Fe. • The Santa Fe lays track from Colorado over Raton Pass, New Mexico, beating the Denver & Rio Grande Railroad by just hours.

1882 • Immigration to the United States peaks, with 105,000 Scandinavians and 250,000 Germans crossing the oceans and heading for western farms.

1883 • Birth of the "Harvey Girl" in Raton, New Mexico.

1888 • Harvey begins to operate dining cars on the Santa Fe between Kansas City and Chicago.

1893 • National depression and other factors force Santa Fe Railroad into receivership.

1896 • A.T. & S.F. purchases the Santa Fe's assets, combining the lines.

1899 • Fred Harvey signs his last contract with the Santa Fe.

1901 • Harvey dies at age 65 in his Leavenworth home. Ford Harvey assumes control of Fred Harvey Company.